THE MAGIC DRUM

Stories from Africa's Savannah, Sea and Skies

Bridget King, Jonti Marks and Gillian Leggat
Illustrated By Robin Miranda

Published by **JACARANDA DESIGNS LTD.**
P.O. Box 76691, Nairobi, Kenya
Copyright © **JACARANDA DESIGNS LTD.**
First Published 1995

Edited by Bridget King
Graphic Design by Katherine Mamai
Cover Design by Robin Miranda

ISBN 9966-884-05-X

Typeset in Belwe, Decollage, and Tekton
Printed in Singapore

THE MAGIC DRUM

Stories from Africa's Savannah, Sea and Skies

Fodo the Frog and the Magic Drum

On the vast plains of Kenya was a place known as 'Kwa Wanyama', or 'Home of the Animals'. A great many animals lived there around a deep waterhole which never dried up. On the banks of the waterhole lived a large, green speckled frog. His name was Fodo.

Fodo was very proud because his grandfather had given him a magic wooden drum. The drum played magic music and everyone who heard it wanted to dance. Every evening, when the sun was low in the sky, Fodo fetched his drum from its secret hiding place in the trunk of an ancient baobab tree.

Sitting on a large rock at the edge of the waterhole where he lived, Fodo played the magic drum and sang a little song:

My name is Fodo
He of the magic drum
Come one, come all,
Come dance to the beat of my drum.

When Hippo heard the magic sound of drumming he lumbered heavily out of the pool. Hippo spent his day wallowing in the cool water so by evening he was very hungry. While the other animals gathered, he

munched and crunched and scrunched the grass at the edge of the pool.

When Elephant, Giraffe, Wildebeest, Impala and Zebra heard the magic sound of drumming they knew it was time to go down to the waterhole.

The monkeys ran down the trees and raced to see who

4

could reach the water first. As the animals enjoyed their evening drink, Fodo played his drum.

"Let's dance," brayed Zebra, kicking up his heels.

"Let's go," trumpeted Elephant, impatient to be off.

"Wait for me," begged shy Impala.

Fodo beat his drum and marched proudly.

As he set off across the plains he croaked in time to the music. The animals followed, trumpeting, braying, snorting and squealing as they danced along behind him.

"It's so clear tonight," croaked Fodo. "Let's go to the edge of the forest.

"Let's dance," brayed Zebra.

"Let's go," trumpeted Elephant.

"Not too far," whispered shy Impala.

Giraffe and Wildebeest nodded their heads. Fodo led the animals across the dry plains and right into the forest. Among the tall trees they saw a shamba, surrounded by a strong fence. Rows of healthy tomatoes, cabbages, spinach and maize grew in the red earth.

"What do I smell?" trumpeted Elephant, raising his trunk up high.

"Maize, delicious maize. I'm so hungry!"

7

Elephant pushed his way through the fence, making a big hole which the others could pass through. He began to rip off the ripest ears of corn. 'Stomp, stomp,' went Elephant's feet as he danced on the spot, flapping his ears happily as he ate the maize.

Wildebeest, Zebra and Impala danced through the hole in the fence. Their noses twitched in delight at the delicious smells. They trotted straight over to a bed of fresh spinach.

"Spinach is much better than the horrid dry grass of the plains," exclaimed Wildebeest as he took a huge mouthful.

"So green and juicy," sighed Impala.

"Hey, hey, hey!" neighed Zebra greedily. "Just watch me eat this whole bed all by myself!"

Hippo sank his huge teeth into a fat cabbage.
"Yum, yum, yum!"

"Hee, hee," laughed the monkeys as they swarmed up into the mango trees. "What enormous mangoes!" they cried. "Sweet, yellow and juicy. A real feast!"

Fodo found a little stream. The water was cool, clear and not too deep. He settled himself on a tree stump and dangled his tired, dusty feet in the water. "What bliss!" he croaked. "The waterhole on the plains is so muddy. This stream is a perfect home for a frog like me. Maybe I shall come and live here." Dreaming of how lovely it would be to live in the cool, clear water, he played his drum.

As the moon began to fade and dawn grew near, the animals plodded heavily back to the plains. Their stomachs were full from eating too much. No one wanted to dance. When at last they reached the waterhole they thanked Fodo for a wonderful night.

"Pretty good for a mere frog," said Elephant

"Let's go back to the shamba tomorrow," brayed Zebra nodding his head.

"Oh yes, let's," smiled shy Impala.

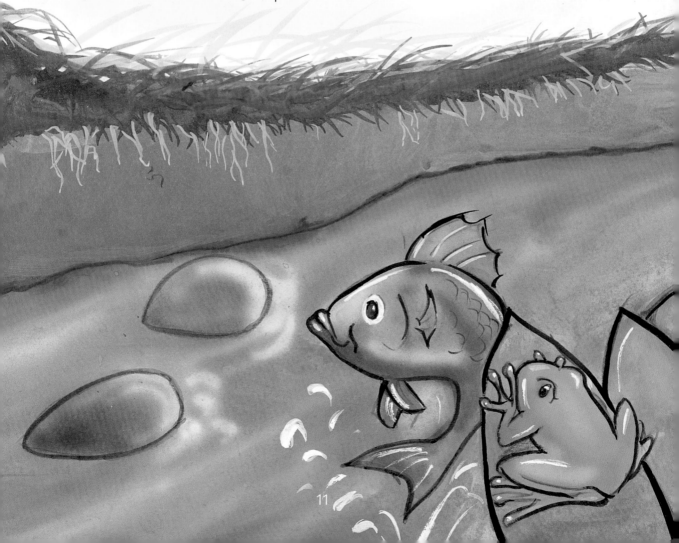

In the morning, the owner of the shamba went to work in his garden. His name was Chunga. When Chunga saw the state of his vegetable garden, he was very, very angry.

"Who's been trampling over my garden?" shouted Chunga in fury. "Who's broken a huge hole in my fence and eaten my best vegetables? I'll find out who's responsible and punish them, just see if I don't."

All day long Chunga worked hard. He mended the hole in the fence, tidied up the beds and smoothed the trampled soil. He cut a strong new club called a 'rungu' and hardened it over a fire. He took out his spear and sharpened the blade. As the sun began to go down, Chunga hid behind his house and waited. He was determined to discover who had caused all the damage.

The animals gathered as Fodo took out his drum that evening.

"Follow me," trumpeted Elephant, impatient to be off. "We're going to the shamba again."

"Oh good," chorused Zebra and Impala. "The spinach was so fresh and tasty." The monkeys swung down from the trees chattering and clapping their hands in glee. "We want to eat more mangoes. Let's go to the shamba," they cried.

As Fodo played his magic drum and the animals marched once more toward the shamba. Elephant broke his way through the fence and one by one the others danced into the garden. Elephant pulled up several stalks of maize with his trunk and began to eat. Wildebeest, Zebra and Impala nibbled at the spinach while Hippo lumbered over to the cabbages. Giraffe danced on her long legs and Fodo marched round and round playing his drum extra loudly.

"STOP!" roared Chunga from behind the hut. "STOP THAT DANCING!" Fodo stopped drumming. Startled, the animals looked up. Frozen in horror, they saw a wild man leap out from behind the hut.

"GET OUT OF MY GARDEN!" roared Chunga again waving his spear and rungu.

In panic the animals scattered. Impala leapt over the fence; Giraffe, Wildebeest and Zebra kicked up their heels and dashed through the hole; Elephant trumpeted, flapping his ears angrily as he followed them; Hippo trotted crossly behind, still munching a huge cabbage which was too tasty to leave behind. Only Fodo was left, rooted to the spot in terror.

"And now for you!" shouted Chunga as he waved his spear at poor Fodo.

Hopping first one way and then the other, Fodo tried desperately to escape. Chunga lashed out with his rungu, just missing Fodo each time. With a giant hop, Fodo jumped through the hole in the fence. He held on tightly to his precious drum, but it was heavy and he couldn't hop very fast. Chasing this way and that, Chunga beat the ground in fury as he ran after Fodo. Fodo hopped and hopped as Chunga ran and ran.

"I'll catch you and cook you for my dinner, you miserable, slimy frog," panted Chunga as he chased Fodo over the plains.

Just as Fodo was
about to drop with
exhaustion, he saw
the moonlight
glinting on the waterhole.

With a last mighty HOP! he leapt into the
water and sank gratefully to the bottom.

"I've missed you this time," Chunga yelled, plunging his spear into the
water in frustration, "but if you ever dare to come back to my shamba,
I'll catch you and your friends!"

Ever since that dreadful night, Fodo has been too terrified to bring his drum out of the water.

In the rainy season, when the waterhole is full and the crops are green, the sound of his under-water drumming can be heard across the plains.

But never from the same place twice. The animals of Kwa Wanyama go to the waterhole every evening, hoping that Fodo will lead them to the shamba again, but he never has. They know Fodo still fears the shamba man and his spear.

Laika
The Crab Who Dreamed Too Much

On the silver shores of Africa there lived a little crab called Laika. Her home was a deep hole on a long white beach of soft coral sand. The beach was gently washed, day after day, by the waves of the Indian Ocean. A soft breeze often came to play among the fringes of the palm trees, making them whisper and giggle in its ticklish wind.

Laika lived with her mother at the foot of a palm tree. At high tide the sea water stopped just before the entrance to their home.

Laika was a dreamer. She spent most of her time sitting in the sun outside the hole thinking of wild beasts and ogres, brave warriors and beautiful young girls. In her favourite day-dream, a handsome prince came to the beach. He fell in love with her and together they went to live in a far-off land.

Laika's mother worried about her dreaming daughter. "Laika," she would say. "You can't spend all your time dreaming. You should find some friends of your own age. Get out more and do things."

"But mother," Laika would answer. "I can hope can't I?"

"Well, yes," said her mother. "But to dream of the impossible is a waste of time. It's much better to hope for something that can happen."

Despite her mother's advice, Laika went on dreaming of the day when her prince would come. Day after day she sat in the sun, dreaming her life away.

Each year, lots of families came to Laika's beach for their holidays. They walked on the sand, played in the sea and enjoyed the warm weather. One day, Laika was sitting outside her hole as usual when three children walked past. Laika didn't pay much attention to them but snatches of their conversation reached her.

"Oh, Rafiki, isn't it beautiful," said a girl's voice.

"It certainly is," replied the boy. "I knew you'd like it."

"If it wasn't for the footprints in the sand," the girl replied, "I'd feel I was the first person ever to come here."

The children moved on down the beach. They hadn't even noticed the little crab sitting at the bottom of the tall palm tree.

To Laika, the effect of their words was electric. Although she hadn't really been listening, one word broke through the clouds of her day-dream. That word was 'footprints'.

"Foot Prince!" thought Laika as a shiver of excitement ran through her. "Foot Prince! Oh goodness! That girl saw a Foot Prince on the beach. He must be looking for me."

She wasn't quite sure how a Foot Prince compared with a normal prince. She imagined it must be a prince who walked everywhere. She didn't care. A prince was a prince, whether he walked or rode. She was sure this prince had come to find her.

"But if he's walking down the beach," she reasoned, "he might miss me. Perhaps he's already gone past my hole and is lost. He may be searching for the crab who loves him."

Laika felt that if she didn't act quickly she would lose her chance. Without a backward glance, without even one thought for her mother, she scuttled away down the long white beach.

"Which way did he go?" she wondered. The thought of her dream prince passing her by made her lose all common sense. She hurried off down the beach as fast as her little legs could carry her.

30

Later, as the sun was beginning to set, Laika's mother came out of the hole. She looked around for her dreamy daughter to call her in for dinner.

"Laika! Food's ready! Come on. I've made your favourite mollusc pie. Oh, that's strange. Where is she? She never goes away from the hole." Mother wondered where Laika had gone. As she searched along the beach she called: "Laika, Laika. Where are you?"

Silence.

It was so unlike her daughter to go missing. Mother Crab began to feel really worried. There were so many dangers in the night. The tide was coming in and the light was almost gone, but there was still no sign of Laika. Calling out Laika's name, Mother Crab searched the beach for her daughter, afraid she was lost in the dark.

32

Meanwhile, Laika had been so keen to find her Foot Prince she hadn't noticed the tide getting higher and higher and the sky growing darker and darker. She stopped to catch her breath. The light had gone from the sky and the high tide changed the shape of the beach. She did not know where she was. Everything looked so different now.

Laika was scared. There was no sign of her Foot Prince and she was lost. Suddenly she felt very frightened and alone. She realised she was very, very small in the huge night around her. The rushing of waves on the shore and rustling of wind in the palm trees seemed unfriendly now.

35

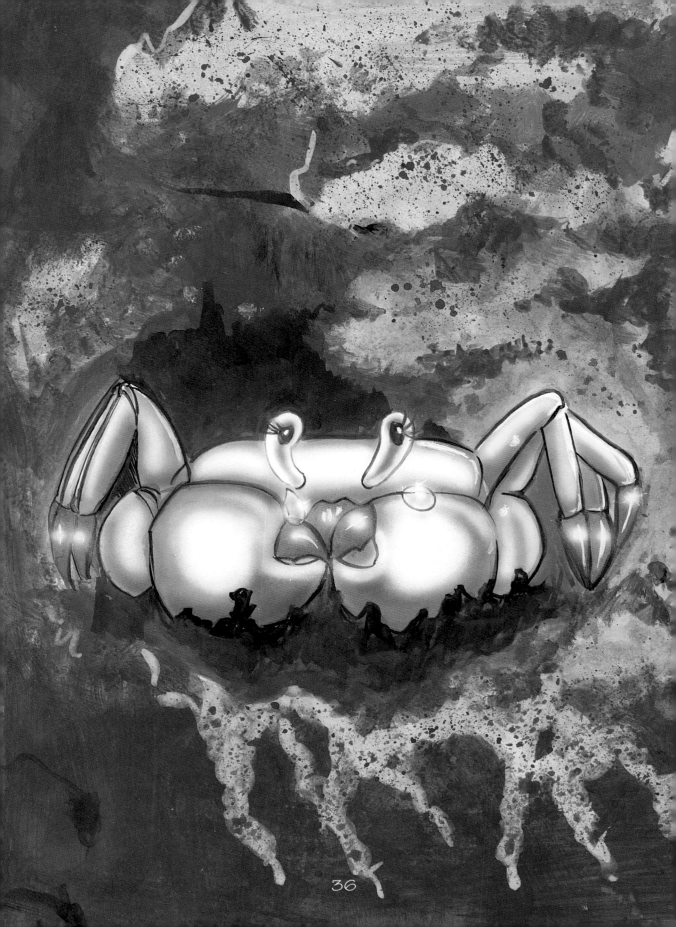

Laika found an overhanging rock, away from the water. She crept into the dark, shivering and shaking as the waves passed around her. As she sheltered from the wind, Laika thought hard about the things that were important to her.

She thought of her beloved home and mother. They were so much more important than her dreams of a perfect prince. Now she couldn't wait to go back home as soon as it was light.

As the sun rose on a new day, Laika was still huddled under the rock. She felt cold, miserable and very foolish. Now that it was light, Laika knew exactly where she was. Quite a long way from home it was true, but not a difficult journey in daylight. Laika set off bravely. She was still some distance away when she saw a familiar figure rushing over the sand towards her. It was her mother, looking worn out after a long night of worry and fear.

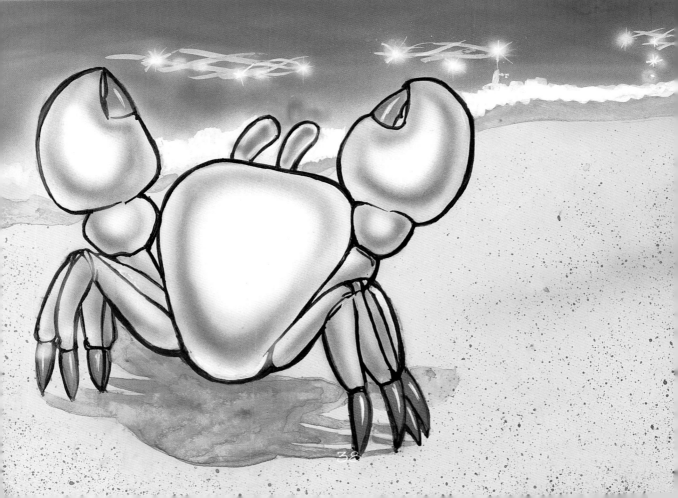

"Oh Mother," said Laika as they hugged each other tightly. "I'm so sorry. I ran off after an empty dream. I'm so ashamed of myself. I just didn't think. I won't do it again, I promise."

Laika's mother said nothing. She hugged her daughter tightly, happy that she was safe. Laika seemed to have learned an important lesson all by herself. It does no harm to dream, but dreams don't always come true. Mother and daughter walked home happily, arm in arm.

Nearly a year has passed since Laika's long, lonely night on the beach. You would hardly recognise her now. She plays with all the crabs of her own age and she is always busy. She no longer spends hours day-dreaming and wishing for things that might never be.

If you ask her now about her Foot Prince she just smiles and says: "Well, maybe he'll come and maybe he won't. Whatever happens, I've got my own life to live." She shrugs and pauses in thought for a moment. With a distant gleam in her eye, she adds: "It would be nice if he did come, though, wouldn't it?"

The Ungrateful Bird

A long time ago Mumba, the creator, made all the animals, birds and plants which live on earth. When it was done, he was very, very tired. He lay down on his favourite cloud and shut his eyes.

Mumba was almost asleep when he was disturbed by a shrill cheeping noise. Turning over onto his side he puffed up his cloud pillow and closed his eyes again. But once more the shrill sound pierced his dreams. With a sigh he rose from his comfortable bed to see who was making the noise. Far below, on the branch of a euphorbia tree, sat a little red bird.

"Cheeeeeeeep, cheeeeeep," it cried, "Cheeeeeeep, cheeeeeeeep."

"Little bird," said Mumba. "Why are you making that noise?"

"Oh, please, Mumba," cheeped the little red bird. "The spotted genet cat is chasing me and I am very frightened."

"Why don't you fly to another tree?" suggested Mumba.

"Even the trees are not safe. The genet waits until I am asleep, then he jumps up the tree to catch me. I am so scared. Cheeeeeeep, cheeeeeeeep. I wish I was a spotted genet."

"You shall have your wish, little bird," said Mumba kindly.

There was a deep roll of thunder. A bright flash of lightning lit up the tree. When it faded a handsome genet cat, with dark brown spots on soft golden fur, sat on the branch. "There," said Mumba. "You have your wish. Now I will go back to my bed."

Mumba settled down comfortably on his fluffy cloud. Beautiful dreams of the earth's new flowers and trees passed before his eyes. The music of the streams and rivers flowed gently through his ears. It was all so peaceful.

Suddenly a loud whine interrupted his slumbers. No! It couldn't possibly be that troublesome bird-genet ,could it? He sat up, rubbed his eyes and peered down at the earth. On the very same branch of the euphorbia tree sat the spotted genet. His sleek coat and sharp claws gleamed in the sunlight.

"Miaaaaauw, miaaaaauw, " it whined.

"Why are you making that noise?" asked Mumba, raising his voice above the din.

"Oh, please, Mumba," begged the genet. "The jackal chased me up this tree. He chased after me and I had to run for my life. I am so afraid."

"But the jackal cannot follow you up the tree," replied Mumba sternly. "Why are you so afraid?"

"I fear I will starve up in this tree. The jackal keeps watch at the bottom and will not let me come down." I wish I were a jackal," moaned the genet.

A bright flash of lightning knocked the genet off the branch onto the ground. Gone was his dark spotted coat and long, sharp claws. Now he had the brownish grey fur, pointed ears and bushy tail of a jackal. Lifting his head, he howled his thanks.

"Now that you have your wish, perhaps you will let me sleep," said Mumba. As he watched the clouds drift past he thought of all the wonderful animals he had created: the ant, the buffalo, the crocodile, the…

A long ghostly howl shattered his pleasant dreams. Three times the howl broke the silence of the evening. At last Mumba could stand it no longer.

"Can that be the bird-genet-jackal animal again? Surely he would not dare disturb my sleep for a third time?"

Mumba stared down and. There in the very same euphorbia tree was the black-backed jackal. The jackal threw back his head and howled again. Until this moment Mumba had been quite patient, but now he grew angry. He put his face right up against the jackal's nose and thundered:

"How dare you disturb my sleep again?"

"Oh, please, Mumba. A mighty lion with enormous claws and sharp teeth chased me," said the jackal. "I had to run faster than I have ever run in my life. If only I were a lion, I would be content. The lion is the king of the beasts.

Once more there was a bright flash of lightning. Straight away a magnificent lion with a golden mane and a handsome face stood before Mumba. The lion roared mightily.

"Now I have changed you into the king of the beasts, " said Mumba. "Go! Roam the land fearlessly and be satisfied with who you are."

Mumba returned to his bed and laid his head on the soft cloudy pillow. "At last I will be able to rest in peace," he sighed. It was good to dream of the great mountains, hills and valleys, the volcanoes, waterfalls and vast seas which covered much of his beautiful earth. He was happy.

Suddenly, a loud roar made his cloud tremble.

"If that is the bird-genet-jackal-lion animal again, he will be in trouble," muttered Mumba. He glared down at the magnificent beast he had so recently created. "You had better give me a good excuse for disturbing my sleep this time," he said angrily.

"Oh, please, Mumba. A fierce man hurled a spear at my shoulder" roared the lion. "The wound is very painful. I wish I were a powerful warrior who all the beasts on earth would fear."

"Your wish will be granted," bellowed Mumba.

Another flash of lightning lit the skies and the lion vanished. In his place stood a tall warrior with feathers in his headdress and a strong shield on his arm. In one hand he held a long spear.

For many moons the warrior was very proud, He fought bravely and brought home herds of fine cattle. One day the king ordered the warrior to give him half his cattle.

"I am a greater man than the king," he said. "Why should I be forced to give him my wealth. The king should be rewarding me for all the cattle I have brought to his land. I will not give him what I have worked so hard to earn. Now, if I were the king, all the warriors in the land would be in my power. I would be happy and wealthy." Turning his face to the sky he called to Mumba, "I wish I were king."

This time a huge column of smoke rose up into the air. The sky went black for a moment and all creatures fell silent. When the smoke cleared, the warrior was seated on the throne, surrounded by his wives and councillors.

For a while the new king was happy. He was rich and well fed. He had people to sing and dance for him. He could tell the other warriors exactly what he wanted them to do and they obeyed his every command. Then one day a messenger arrived.

"I bring a message from Mumba," said the messenger. "You must bow down and make sacrifices to him, for he is Lord of the Universe."

"I will not bow down," shouted the king in anger. "I will not make sacrifices to him. I am the most powerful king in the world. I bow to nobody."

61

Suddenly a strong wind blew, lifting off the roof of the king's house. Bolts of lightning flashed across the sky and thunder crashed overhead. When the storm died down the terrified councillors opened their eyes and looked around. They were puzzled.

Just a moment ago their king had been sitting on his throne. Now all they could see was a little red bird which sang "Cheeeeeeep, cheeeeep."

As they watched, the little red bird flew away and was never seen again.

Meet the Authors

Bridget King

Born in Kent, England, Bridget first came to Africa in 1973 after taking a BEd degree in Ceramics and Comparative Education. She has since worked in Zambia, Somalia, Lesotho and Kenya as an art teacher, a freelance photo-journalist and is currently Managing Editor for Jacaranda Designs. Her love of story telling came from her father who brought her up with stories of his life in Africa. She has two daughters.

Gillian Leggat

Gillian is a South African living in Natal with a BA Degree in English and Psychology and a MA Degree in English. Most of her experience has been in the field of educational supplementary reading books for the black schools market. Since 1989 she has been published extensively and her stories have been produced by South African Broadcasting Company for children's television.

Jonti Marks

Also born in England, Jonti was educated in Nairobi and spent the first two decades of his life between Africa and Europe. Jonti has been a keen writer from an early age and now, as the father of two young children he finds plenty of inspiration and a ready audience for his short stories. He has made his home in Kenya and is a dedicated teacher.

Meet the Artist

Robin Miranda

Robin is of Goan origin, although he was born and brought up entirely in Kenya. He is one of seven children with three brothers and three sisters. At 33 years old Robin is unmarried but has twelve nieces and nephews who are often with him, pleading for him to draw them pictures and cartoons! Mainly self-taught, Robin has developed an enviable reputation for his illustrative talent. He works as a freelance artist in the Jacaranda complex, but has his own studio set apart from the main office.

So far Robin has worked on two titles in the Mcheshi series: **Mcheshi Goes on a Journey** and **Mcheshi Goes to School.** Robin accompanies the Mcheshi team on their research field trips so that he knows the background as fully as the writers and other artists. In this series, Robin composes the outline sketches with co-illustrator Judy Mathenge.

The Magic Drum is a book of three stories from the savannah, sea and sky of Kenya and South Africa, entirely illustrated by Robin. This book is his third title fully illustrated by him, the first being **The Great Greedy Ogre** and the second **The Secret of The Mango Grove** in our Kidogo Collection.

Robin works in most media, but is an airbrush technique specialist, a skill which he has taught to other artists in the company. In his spare time, Robin teaches Bible Studies and is keen to keep fit by exercising.